"Review of the President's Fiscal Year 2016 Funding Request for the Department of the Treasury and the Internal Revenue Service"

Washington, D.C.

TESTIMONY
OF
THE HONORABLE J. RUSSELL GEORGE
TREASURY INSPECTOR GENERAL FOR TAX ADMINISTRATION
before the
COMMITTEE ON APPROPRIATIONS, SUBCOMMITTEE ON
FINANCIAL SERVICES AND GENERAL GOVERNMENT
UNITED STATES SENATE

"Review of the President's Fiscal Year 2016 Funding Request for the Department of the Treasury and the Internal Revenue Service"

March 3, 2015

Chairman Boozman, Ranking Member Coons, and Members of the Subcommittee, thank you for the opportunity to testify on the Internal Revenue Service's (IRS) Fiscal Year (FY)[1] 2016 budget request, our recent work related to the most significant challenges currently facing the IRS, and the Treasury Inspector General for Tax Administration's (TIGTA) FY 2016 budget request.

The Treasury Inspector General for Tax Administration, also known as "TIGTA," is statutorily mandated to provide independent audit and investigative services necessary to improve the economy, efficiency, and effectiveness of the IRS, including the IRS Chief Counsel and the IRS Oversight Board. TIGTA's oversight activities are designed to identify high-risk systemic inefficiencies in IRS operations and to investigate exploited weaknesses in tax administration. TIGTA's role is critical in that we provide the American taxpayer with assurance that the approximately 91,000[2] IRS employees, who collected over $3.1 trillion in tax revenue, processed over 242 million tax returns and other forms, and issued $374 billion in tax refunds[3] during FY 2014, perform their duties in an effective and efficient manner while minimizing the risks of waste, fraud, or abuse.

OVERVIEW OF THE IRS'S FY 2016 BUDGET REQUEST

The IRS is the largest component of the Department of the Treasury and has primary responsibility for administering the Federal tax system. The IRS's budget

---

[1] The Federal Government's fiscal year begins on October 1 and ends on September 30.
[2] Total IRS staffing as of January 24, 2015. Included in the total are approximately 19,000 seasonal and part-time employees.
[3] IRS, *Management's Discussion & Analysis, Fiscal Year 2014*, page 2.

request supports the Department of the Treasury's Strategic Goal of fairly and effectively reforming and modernizing Federal financial management, accounting and tax systems and the Department of the Treasury Agency Priority Goal of increasing self-service and electronic service options for taxpayers.

The IRS Strategic Plan for FY 2014-2017 provides a central direction for the agency and guides program and budget decisions. The IRS's strategic goals are to: 1) deliver high quality and timely service to reduce taxpayer burden and encourage voluntary compliance, and 2) effectively enforce the law to ensure compliance with tax responsibilities and combat fraud. To achieve these goals, the proposed FY 2016 IRS budget requests appropriated resources of approximately $12.9 billion.[4] The total appropriation amount is an increase of $2 billion, or approximately 18 percent more than the FY 2015 enacted level of approximately $10.9 billion. This increase is illustrated in Table 1. The budget request includes a net staffing increase of 9,245 Full-Time Equivalents (FTE)[5] for a total of approximately 90,524 appropriated FTEs.

---

[4] The FY 2016 budget request also includes approximately $127 million from reimbursable programs, $33 million from non-reimbursable programs, $450 million from user fees, $386 million in available unobligated funds from prior years, and a transfer of $5 million to the Alcohol and Tobacco Tax and Trade Bureau for a total amount of $13.9 billion in available resources.
[5] A measure of labor hours in which one FTE is equal to eight hours multiplied by the number of compensable days in a particular fiscal year.

TABLE 1
IRS FY 2016 Budget Request Increase
Over FY 2015 Enacted Budget
(in Thousands)

Appropriations Account	FY 2015 Enacted	FY 2016 Request	$ Change	% Change
Taxpayer Services	$2,156,554	$2,408,803	$252,249	11.7%
Enforcement	$4,860,000	$5,399,832	$539,832	11.1%
Operations Support	$3,638,446	$4,743,258	$1,104,812	30.4%
Business Systems Modernization	$290,000	$379,178	$89,178	30.8%
Total Appropriated Resources	$10,945,000	$12,931,071	$1,986,071	18.2%

Source: Treasury Inspector General for Tax Administration's analysis of the IRS's FY 2016 Budget Request, Operating Level Tables.

The three largest appropriation accounts are Taxpayer Services, Enforcement, and Operations Support. The Taxpayer Services account provides funding for programs that focus on helping taxpayers understand and meet their tax obligations, while the Enforcement account supports the IRS's examination and collection efforts. The Operations Support account provides funding for functions that are essential to the overall operation of the IRS, such as infrastructure and information services. Finally, the Business Systems Modernization account provides funding for the development of new tax administration systems and investments in electronic filing.

As shown in Table 1, the Operations Support budget request for FY 2016 increased by over 30 percent or $1.1 billion and 1,820 FTE compared to FY 2015. The three largest components driving this increase are as follows:

- $495 million (975 FTE) for Information Technology changes related to the Affordable Care Act and other requirements to sustain critical information technology infrastructure;
- $118 million (164 FTE) for improved taxpayer service and return processing, including efforts to address the projected growth in demand for traditional taxpayer services as well as to improve taxpayer assistance;
- $85 million (74 FTE) for consolidating and modernizing IRS facilities, including reducing office space to realize an estimated annual rent savings of $23 million.

REDUCTIONS IN THE IRS'S FY 2015 BUDGET

The IRS's appropriated funding was reduced by $346 million over the last year, from $11.3 billion in the FY 2014 enacted budget to $10.9 billion in FY 2015. To address this, the IRS reduced planned spending in a variety of key areas for FY 2015. The areas with the largest cuts are total personnel compensation ($142 million), equipment ($65 million), communication and utilities ($55 million), and operation and maintenance of equipment ($42 million). The IRS also reduced overall net spending on services by $40 million.[6] Finally, the IRS had an exception-only hiring freeze in place during FY 2014 which also remains in place in FY 2015.

Even with these reductions, the IRS Commissioner testified on February 3, 2015[7] that the IRS still faces a significant budget shortfall for FY 2015. As a result, the IRS is planning for the possibility of a shutdown of IRS operations for two days later this fiscal year, which will involve furloughing employees on those days. The IRS Commissioner also testified that these budget cuts will have negative impacts on taxpayer service and enforcement. For example, the Commissioner stated the IRS will delay replacement of aging information technology systems, increasing the risk of downtime and negatively affecting taxpayer service. In addition, the Commissioner indicated reduced staffing will result in decreased audits and collection activities, as well as delays in customer service during the 2015 filing season.

---

[6] The overall net reduction in services includes a decrease of $100.2 million in other services from non-federal sources and an increase of $60.3 million in advisory and assistance services.

[7] Written Testimony of John A. Koskinen, Commissioner of the IRS, before the Senate Finance Committee, dated February 3, 2015.

CHALLENGES FACING THE IRS

Achieving program efficiencies and cost savings is imperative, as the IRS must continue to carry out its mission with a significantly reduced budget. TIGTA reported that implementation of the mandated sequestration,[8] coupled with a trend of lower budgets, reduced staffing, and the loss of supplementary funding for the implementation of the Patient Protection and Affordable Care Act of 2010 and the Health Care and Education Reconciliation Act of 2010 (collectively referred to as the Affordable Care Act or ACA)[9] affected the IRS's ability to deliver its priority program areas, including customer service and enforcement activities.[10]

For example, the IRS's toll-free Level of Service[11] decreased from 68 percent in FY 2012 to 61 percent in FY 2013. As of February 14, 2015, more than 26 million taxpayers contacted the IRS during the 2015 Filing Season by calling various Accounts Management toll-free telephone assistance lines[12] seeking help to understand the tax law and meet their tax obligations. The IRS answered more than 9.3 million calls through automated scripts and more than 2.6 million calls by an IRS assistor. The Average Speed of Answer for an IRS assistor-answered telephone call was 28 minutes. As of February 14, 2015, the IRS reported a 43 percent Level of Service for calls answered by an assistor. In addition, as of February 14, 2015, the over-age correspondence inventory totaled more than 1.3 million.

Key examination and collection statistics also declined. Examinations of individual tax returns decreased approximately five percent from FY 2012 to FY 2013. In addition, collection activities initiated by the IRS, such as liens, levies, and property seizures, decreased approximately 33 percent during the same period. Our analysis of select customer service and enforcement statistics indicates that the downward trend in these areas may continue.

For example, budget cuts have resulted in significant declines in the IRS

---

[8] Sequestration involves automatic spending cuts of approximately $1 trillion across the Federal Government that took effect on March 1, 2013.

[9] Pub. L. No. 111-148, 124 Stat. 119 (2010) (codified as amended in scattered sections of Internal Revenue Code and 42 U.S.C.), as amended by the Heath Care and Education Reconciliation Act of 2010, Pub. L. No. 111-152, 124 Stat. 1029.

[10] TIGTA, Ref. No. 2014-10-025, *Implementation of Fiscal Year 2013 Sequestration Budget Reductions* (June 2014).

[11] The primary measure of service to taxpayers. It is the relative success rate of taxpayers who call for live assistance on the IRS's toll-free telephone lines.

[12] The IRS refers to the suite of 29 telephone lines to which taxpayers can make calls as "Customer Account Services Toll-Free."

collection program.[13] From FY 2010 to FY 2014, the budgets for the Automated Collection System (ACS)[14] operations and Field Collection were reduced by over $269 million. ACS staffing has been reduced by 24 percent since FY 2011, and the number of revenue officers has decreased 24 percent since FY 2011. As a result, in FY 2014 revenue officers closed 34 percent fewer cases and collected $222 million less than in FY 2011. ACS contact representatives answered 25 percent fewer calls in FY 2014 than in FY 2011 and collected $224 million less in FY 2014 than in FY 2011.

At the same time the IRS is operating with a reduced budget, it continues to shoulder increased responsibilities as it implements and administers provisions of the Affordable Care Act. This filing season represents the first time taxpayers must report on their tax returns whether they and their dependents maintained minimum essential health care insurance coverage or face a tax penalty for not maintaining this coverage. The IRS must also ensure that the more than six million individuals who purchased insurance from a Health Care Exchange[15] accurately reconcile on their tax returns advance payments of the Premium Tax Credit (PTC)[16] they may have received.

Since enactment of the Affordable Care Act, these responsibilities have required the IRS to develop new information technology, modify existing computer systems, and establish new or revised filing, reporting, and compliance processes and procedures. The IRS's FY 2016 budget request includes $490 million to fund 2,539 FTEs for continued efforts related to the implementation of ACA. The largest components of this increase are $306 million to implement information technology changes to deliver ACA tax credits; $101 million to improve taxpayer service and return processing; and $67 million to address the impact of new ACA statutory requirements.

In addition, the IRS continues to dedicate significant resources to detect and review potential identity theft tax returns as well as to assist victims. Resources have not been sufficient for the IRS to work identity theft cases dealing with refund fraud, which continues to be a concern. IRS employees who work the majority of identity theft

---

[13] TIGTA, Audit No. 201330013, *Budget Cuts Resulted in Significant Declines in Key Resources and Unfavorable Trends in Collection Program Performance*, report planned for April 2015.

[14] The Automated Collection System consists of 15 call sites with contact representatives to engage taxpayers and their representatives on resolving unpaid tax debts. Field Collection consists of over 400 offices across the country through which revenue officers contact taxpayers in person to resolve tax debts and secure unfiled returns.

[15] Exchanges are intended to allow eligible individuals to obtain health insurance, and all Exchanges, whether State-based or established and operated by the Federal government, are required to perform certain functions.

[16] A refundable tax credit to assist individuals and families in purchasing health insurance coverage through an Affordable Insurance Exchange.

cases are telephone assistors who also respond to taxpayers' calls to the IRS's toll-free telephone lines. This has contributed to the IRS's inability to timely resolve victims' cases as well as the continued decline in its ability to respond to taxpayers' written correspondence. The allocation of limited resources requires difficult decisions, with a focus on balancing taxpayer assistance on the toll-free telephone lines during the filing season with other various priority programs, such as identity theft and aged work.

For example, the IRS previously reallocated ACS staff, who attempt to collect taxes through telephone contact with taxpayers, to work the growing inventory of identity theft cases. The combination of fewer resources and the need to continue answering telephone calls has contributed to trends that have been unfavorable to several ACS business results over the past four years. Specifically, we determined that inventory is growing because new inventory is outpacing case closures; cases in inventory are aging because inventory is taking longer to close; revenue declined while more cases were closed as uncollectible; and fewer enforcement actions (liens and levies) were taken.[17]

During the past several years, the IRS has continued to take steps to more effectively detect and prevent the issuance of fraudulent refunds resulting from identity theft tax return filings. The IRS reported that in Filing Season 2013, its efforts prevented between $22 billion and $24 billion in identity theft tax refunds from being issued.[18] This is a result of the IRS's continued enhancement of filters used to detect tax returns with a high likelihood of involving identity theft at the time the returns are processed. For example, the IRS used 11 filters in Processing Year (PY) 2012 to identify tax returns with a high likelihood of involving identity theft, compared to 114 filters used in PY 2014. The use of these filters assists the IRS in more effectively allocating its resources to address identity theft tax refund fraud.

The IRS has also taken steps to more effectively prevent the filing of identity theft tax returns by locking the tax accounts of deceased individuals to prevent others from filing a tax return using their name and Social Security Number. The IRS has locked approximately 26.3 million taxpayer accounts between January 2011 and December 31, 2014. In addition, the IRS issues an Identity Protection Personal Identification Number (IP PIN) to any taxpayer who is a confirmed victim of identity theft or who has reported to the IRS that he or she could be at risk of identity theft. Once the IRS confirms the identity of a victim or "at-risk" taxpayer, the IRS will issue the taxpayer

---

[17] TIGTA, Ref. No. 2014-30-080, *Declining Resources Have Contributed to Unfavorable Trends in Several Key Automated Collection System Business Results* (Sep. 2014).
[18] IRS Identity Theft Taxonomy, dated September 15, 2014, page 1.

an IP PIN for use by the taxpayer when filing his or her tax return. The presence of a valid IP PIN on the tax return tells the IRS that the rightful taxpayer filed the tax return, thus reducing the need for the IRS to screen the tax return for potential identity theft. The IRS has issued more than 1.5 million IP PINs for PY 2015.

Despite these improvements, the IRS recognizes that new identity theft patterns are constantly evolving and, as such, it needs to adapt its detection and prevention processes. The IRS's own analysis estimates that identity thieves were successful in receiving over $5 billion in fraudulent tax refunds in Filing Season 2013. This will require the continued expenditure of resources that could otherwise be used to respond to taxpayer telephone calls, answer correspondence, and resolve discrepancies on tax returns.

In addition, TIGTA reported that not all eligible individuals are receiving an IP PIN and victims continue to experience delays and errors in receiving refunds. Specifically, we reported that the IRS did not provide an IP PIN to 557,265 eligible taxpayers for PY 2013.[19] Excluding eligible taxpayers from the IP PIN program will delay IRS processing of their tax returns and receipt of their tax refund. We also reported that the IRS continues to make errors on the tax accounts of victims of identity theft.[20] These errors further delayed refunds issued to taxpayers and required the IRS to reopen cases and expend limited resources to resolve the errors.

Another challenging area is the ongoing IRS impersonation scam. Between October 2013 and January 31, 2015, TIGTA has logged approximately 300,000 contacts from taxpayers who reported that they received telephone calls from individuals claiming to be IRS employees. The impersonators told the victims that they owed additional tax and, if the tax was not immediately paid, they would be arrested, lose their driver's licenses, or face other consequences. As of January 31, 2015, more than 3,000 victims have reported an aggregate loss in excess of $15 million dollars. While TIGTA investigates these complaints, we have worked closely with the IRS, the Federal Trade Commission and local media outlets to publish press releases, warnings, and other public awareness announcements in order to warn taxpayers of the scam. The sheer volume of contacts from concerned taxpayers is an additional strain on IRS resources.

The IRS must continue to identify and implement innovative and cost-saving

---

[19] TIGTA, Ref. No. 2014-40-086, *Identity Protection Personal Identification Numbers Are Not Provided to All Eligible Taxpayers* (Sep. 2014).
[20] TIGTA, Audit No. 201340036, *Identity Theft Victim Assistance – Follow-Up*, report planned for March 2015.

strategies to accomplish its mission of providing America's taxpayers with top-quality service by helping them understand and meet their tax responsibilities and enforce the law with integrity and fairness.

EFFECTIVENESS AND EFFICIENCY OF THE IRS

While the IRS faces many challenges, TIGTA has recently reported on several other areas where the IRS can achieve cost savings, more efficiently use its limited resources, and make more informed business decisions. In addition, timelier reporting of third-party data and additional authority would assist the IRS in improving tax administration.

Opportunities Exist for Additional Cost Savings

In August 2012, TIGTA reported that the IRS can achieve additional cost savings by better managing its real property costs. TIGTA reported that the IRS completed 17 space consolidation and relocation projects from October 2010 through December 2011, which the IRS estimated would result in $2.8 million of realized rent savings in FY 2012. However, we reported that the IRS continues to incur rental costs for more workstations than required. TIGTA estimated that if the employees the IRS allows to routinely telework on a full- or part-time basis shared their workstations on days they were not in the office, 10,244 workstations could potentially be eliminated. The sharing of these workstations could allow the IRS to reduce its long-term office space needs by almost one million square feet, resulting in potential rental savings of approximately $111 million over five years. The IRS agreed with our recommendations and indicated it would revise interim and long-range portfolio strategies for future space needs at sites to include workstation sharing as appropriate.[21]

In September 2014, TIGTA also reported that potential cost savings could be achieved from expanded electronic filing of business returns.[22] IRS efforts have resulted in considerable growth in the electronic filing of individual tax returns, which stood at an 81 percent rate in PY 2012. In comparison, the electronic filing rate of business tax returns in Tax Year (TY) 2012 was 41 percent. Employment tax returns provide the most significant opportunity for growth in business electronic filing. For TY 2012, more than 21.1 million (71 percent) employment tax returns were paper-filed. The Electronic Federal Tax Payment System (EFTPS) has been used in

---

[21] TIGTA, Ref. No. 2012-10-100, *Significant Additional Real Estate Cost Savings Can Be Achieved by Implementing a Telework Workstation Sharing Strategy* (Aug. 2012).
[22] TIGTA, Ref. No. 2014-40-084, *A Service-Wide Strategy Is Needed to Increase Business Tax Return Electronic Filing* (Sep. 2014).

the past to facilitate the e-filing of employment tax returns for Federal agencies. TIGTA recommended that the IRS consider this option for business taxpayers. Providing businesses the ability to electronically file their tax returns concurrently with payment of their tax due on the same system could provide one-stop service which would benefit business filers.

The IRS did not agree to implement this recommendation and offered as an explanation that the Modernized e-File system has been established as the system for receiving employment tax returns electronically. This system provides taxpayers with the ability to remit tax payments when submitting their returns. Notwithstanding this explanation, the implementation of this system has not resulted in a significant increase in the e-filing rate for these tax returns. Moreover, this system does not accept quarterly employment tax deposits.

In September 2014, TIGTA reported that the IRS does not effectively manage server software licenses and is not adhering to Federal requirements and industry best practices. Until the IRS addresses these issues, it will continue to incur increased risks in managing software licenses. TIGTA estimates that the inadequate management of server software licenses potentially costs the Government between $81 million and $114 million, based on amounts spent for licenses and annual license maintenance that were not being used.[23] While the IRS agreed with our recommendation to improve the management of server software licenses, it believes it has subsequently mitigated some of these issues.

Finally, TIGTA estimates that the IRS may have issued more than $439 million in potentially erroneous tax refunds claimed on 187,421 amended returns in FY 2012. Currently, amended tax returns can only be filed on paper and are manually processed. TIGTA's review of a statistical sample of 259 amended tax returns identified 44 tax returns (17 percent) with questionable claims. TIGTA reported that the processes the IRS uses to verify originally filed tax returns would have identified most of the 44 questionable amended returns TIGTA identified as needing additional scrutiny before the refund was paid. TIGTA forecasts using these same processes could prevent the issuance of more than $2.1 billion in erroneous refunds associated with amended tax returns over the next five years. In addition, TIGTA reported that the IRS could have potentially saved $17 million in FY 2012 if it allowed taxpayers to electronically file

---

[23] TIGTA, Ref. No. 2014-20-042, *The Internal Revenue Service Should Improve Server Software Asset Management and Reduce Costs* (Sep. 2014).

amended tax returns.[24] The IRS agreed with TIGTA's recommendation to expand electronic filing of amended tax returns.

The IRS Could Take Actions to More Efficiently Use Its Limited Resources

TIGTA has identified other opportunities for the IRS to more efficiently use its available resources. For example, TIGTA identified potential improvements in the efficiency of the ACS.[25] The ACS plays an integral role in the IRS's efforts to collect unpaid taxes and secure unfiled tax returns. ACS employees are responsible for collecting unpaid taxes and securing tax returns from delinquent taxpayers who have not complied with previous notices. The number of ACS contact representatives in FY 2013 was 39 percent less than in FY 2010 due either to attrition or reassignment, and these resources are needed to answer incoming telephone calls and work identity theft cases. This resulted in fewer resources available to devote to the collection of unpaid taxes. However, the IRS's overall collection inventory practices were not changed to reflect the reduced workforce and, as a result, new inventory continued to be sent to the ACS without interruption, even though inventory was infrequently worked. This has had a substantial impact on the amount of Federal taxes that remain uncollected.

The IRS agreed with our recommendations to re-examine the ACS's role in the collection workflow process, including inventory delivery to the ACS as well as case retention criteria, and to align ACS resources accordingly. In addition, the IRS also agreed to establish performance metrics for ACS call data to measure the impact that answering taxpayer calls has on compliance business results. Capturing these data could allow ACS management to assess the impact of prioritizing call handling versus working inventory and of limiting enforcement actions in order to reduce the volume of incoming calls to the ACS.

TIGTA also found that the IRS's fieldwork collection process is not designed to ensure that cases with the highest collection potential are identified, selected, and assigned to be worked.[26] Although the IRS has begun some initiatives intended to

---

[24] TIGTA, Ref. No. 2014-40-028, *Amended Tax Return Filing and Processing Needs to Be Modernized to Reduce Erroneous Refunds, Processing Costs, and Taxpayer Burden* (Apr. 2014).
[25] TIGTA, Ref. No. 2014-30-080, *Declining Resources Have Contributed to Unfavorable Trends in Several Key Automated Collection System Business Results* (Sep. 2014).
[26] The IRS's Collection function has the primary responsibility for collecting delinquent taxes and tax returns while ensuring that taxpayer rights are protected.

improve the workload selection process, TIGTA believes further action is warranted.[27] With significant growth in delinquent accounts and a reduction in the number of employees, it is essential that the field inventory selection process identifies the cases that have the highest risk and potential for collection.

TIGTA is currently following up on our recommendations regarding inappropriate criteria the IRS used to identify organizations applying for tax-exempt status for review in the area of political campaign intervention. TIGTA has determined that the IRS has taken significant actions to (1) eliminate the selection of potential political cases based on names and policy positions, (2) expedite processing of Internal Revenue Code Section 501(c)(4) social welfare applications, and (3) eliminate unnecessary information requests.[28]

Better Processes and Information Would Assist the IRS in Making Informed Decisions

TIGTA has also identified areas in which the IRS could make more informed business decisions when determining how to use its limited resources. For example, the IRS eliminated or reduced services at Taxpayer Assistance Centers, or TACs. This move was completed to balance taxpayer demand for services with the IRS's anticipated budget cuts, redirect taxpayers to online services, enable assistors to dedicate more time to answer tax account-related inquiries, and offer other services at the TACs, such as identity theft services and acceptance of payments. Although the IRS stated that the services eliminated or reduced were, in part, the result of the IRS's anticipated budget cuts, TIGTA reported that the IRS's plans did not show to what extent the service cuts would lower the costs.

The services the IRS reduced or eliminated at the TACs include preparation of tax returns, refund inquiries, transcript requests, and assistance with tax law questions.[29] These services were reduced or eliminated without evaluating the burden that the changes would have on the low-income, elderly, and limited-English-proficient taxpayers who seek face-to-face service. For example, management decided to stop providing tax transcripts at the TACs, informing customers that they should use its online application "Get Transcript." However, this decision was made with no analysis

---

[27] TIGTA, Ref. No. 2014-30-068, *Field Collection Could Work Cases With Better Collection Potential* (Sep. 2014).
[28] TIGTA, Audit Number 201410009, *Status of Actions Taken to Improve the Processing of Tax-Exempt Applications Involving Political Campaign Intervention*, report planned for April 2015.
[29] TIGTA, Ref. No. 2014-40-038, *Processes to Determine Optimal Face-to-Face Taxpayer Services, Locations, and Virtual Services Have Not Been Established* (June 2014).

of the anticipated increase in traffic to this online application to ensure that it could meet the increased demand. In February 2014, IRS management modified its plan to stop providing transcripts at the TACs, based on concerns about the expected volume of online requests for transcripts as well as concerns raised regarding the launch of another Federal Government website. Management subsequently changed its position, alerting assistors at the TACs to encourage taxpayers to use the "Get Transcript" application but also indicated it will not turn away taxpayers who request transcripts.

Furthermore, we reported that a process has not been developed to expand Virtual Service Delivery, which integrates video and audio technology to allow taxpayers to see and hear an assistor located at remote locations. Taxpayers can use this technology to obtain many of the services available at the TACs. The IRS's stated goals for Virtual Service Delivery are to enhance the use of IRS resources, optimize staffing, and balance its workload. We recommended that the IRS establish a process to identify the best locations for virtual face-to-face services. However, the IRS did not agree to follow through on this recommendation because, in its view, it has established a process to identify the best locations for virtual face-to-face services. However, we believe that the IRS's geographic coverage methodology does not identify optimal underserved areas across the country that would benefit the most from Virtual Service Delivery expansion.

TIGTA also found that the IRS's use of cost/benefit information in managing its enforcement resources could be significantly improved.[30] The allocation of enforcement resources represents an increasingly complex challenge for the IRS in light of significant reductions in its budget. Return on investment (ROI) information, including both estimated ROI for new enforcement initiatives and cost/benefit calculations based on actual program results and costs, is an important tool available to assist IRS senior executives in managing enforcement resources. Although cost/benefit information is considered in making resource allocation decisions, the IRS does not document how or to what extent it uses the information and has no policies or procedures to guide this process. TIGTA also found that the IRS continues to be unable to measure actual revenue from new enforcement initiatives funded in prior years.

---

[30] TIGTA, Ref. No. 2013-10-104, *The Use of Return on Investment Information in Managing Tax Enforcement Resources Could Be Improved* (Sep. 2013).

We also determined that the IRS's processes do not ensure that corporations accurately claim carryforward general business credits.[31] During PY 2013, corporate filers claimed more than $93 billion in general business credits. These credits offset taxes owed by more than $21 billion. TIGTA identified 3,285 e-filed Forms 1120, *U.S. Corporation Income Tax Return*, filed in PY 2013 on which corporations claimed potentially erroneous carryforward credits totaling more than $2.7 billion. We recommended the IRS develop processes to address the deficiencies identified in our report. The IRS does not plan to implement this recommendation due to lack of information technology resources and competing priorities.

In addition, TIGTA recently reported that the IRS hired some former employees with prior substantiated conduct or performance issues.[32] The practice of rehiring former employees with known conduct and performance issues presents increased risk to the IRS and taxpayers. For example, TIGTA found that nearly 20 percent of the rehired former employees TIGTA sampled who had prior substantiated or unresolved conduct or performance issues also had new conduct or performance issues after being rehired. This is significant because the time spent by IRS managers addressing performance and conduct issues is time taken away from serving taxpayers and enforcing the law.

The IRS is also dedicating significant resources toward addressing what it believes to be the most significant risks to compliance, such as the challenge presented by taxpayers' increasing use of flow-through entities, such as partnerships.[33] In the IRS's 2014–2017 Strategic Plan,[34] one of its stated goals is to ensure compliance with tax responsibilities and to combat fraud, and one of its stated measures of success is an increase in voluntary compliance by three percent from 83 percent to 86 percent by 2017.

TIGTA continues to audit the efficiency and effectiveness of the IRS's efforts to reduce the Tax Gap[35] and improve voluntary tax compliance. In the area of partnership compliance, for example, the IRS initiated its Partnership Strategy in July 2012 to

---

[31] The general business credit is offered as an incentive for a business to engage in certain kinds of activities considered beneficial to the economy or the public at large and is used to reduce a corporation's regular tax liability. A carryforward is the amount of the general business credit that is unused because of the tax liability limit for claiming the credit.

[32] TIGTA, Ref. No. 2015-10-006, *Additional Consideration of Prior Conduct and Performance Issues Is Needed When Hiring Former Employees* (Dec. 2014).

[33] Between 2008 and 2012, the number of business partnership filings increased by 21 percent.

[34] IRS Strategic Plan FY 2014-2017.

[35] The Tax Gap is the difference between what all taxpayers owe and what they pay. The IRS estimated the net tax gap (after factoring in forced collections) to be approximately $385 billion annually.

improve the partnership audit process in light of the significant increase in partnership filings and complexities associated with auditing partnership returns. TIGTA recently completed a review of the partnership audit program and found that the IRS has no effective way to assess the productivity of its partnership audits since many complex partnerships have multiple layers of flow-through entities.[36] In order to track partnership audits, the IRS uses a decade's old system that is unable to provide information on the total amount of taxes that are ultimately assessed to the taxable partners as a result of adjustments made to the partnership returns. Therefore, the IRS is unable to assess the full impact of its partnership compliance activities.

The IRS agrees that this is a significant problem but asserts that a new information technology system is the only means to obtain the necessary information on the productivity of its partnership compliance program. Until such time as the IRS upgrades its systems, TIGTA believes the IRS could make better use of the significant research capacity within the IRS to address this formidable tax compliance challenge. Although the IRS has requested over $16 million as part of its FY 2016 budget request to increase the number of agents with specialized experience in auditing large partnerships, it has not taken the steps to improve the tracking of the results of its partnership audits so that it can make the best use of its resources devoted to this area.

More Timely Third-Party Reporting and Correctable Error Authority

Each year, the IRS receives information returns filed by third parties such as employers and educational institutions. These returns provide the IRS the information needed to verify taxpayers' claims for benefits such as the Earned Income Tax Credit (EITC) and the American Opportunity Tax Credit (AOTC). However, information returns are generally not filed with the IRS until after most taxpayers file their annual tax returns. As a result, the IRS cannot use the information contained on these information returns to verify tax returns until after those tax returns are processed and refunds are issued.

For example, the IRS estimates that in FY 2013, 30 percent of (or $4.35 billion) in improper EITC payments resulted from verification errors associated with the IRS's inability to identify taxpayers who misreport their income to erroneously claim the EITC. TIGTA's review of TY 2012 tax returns identified more than $1.7 billion in potentially erroneous EITC claims on tax returns for which no third-party Forms W-2, *Wage and Tax Statement*, supporting the wages reported had been received by the IRS.

---

[36] TIGTA, Audit No. 201430027, *Additional Improvements Are Needed to Measure the Success and Productivity of the Partnership Audit Process*, report planned for March 2015.

However, the IRS does not have the Forms W-2 information at the time most of these tax returns are processed. Employers who file paper Forms W-2 are not required to file these forms until February of each year. Employers who e-file Forms W-2 have until the end of March each year to file.

TIGTA also estimates that the IRS issued more than $3.2 billion in potentially erroneous education credits in TY 2012 for students for whom the IRS did not receive a Form 1098-T, *Tuition Statement*, from a postsecondary educational institution.[37] Educational institutions are required to provide a Form 1098-T to students who attend their institution and file a copy of Form 1098-T with the IRS. The Form 1098-T provides the name and Employer Identification Number of the institution, the name and Taxpayer Identification Number of the student who attended, and information on whether the student attended half-time or was a graduate student. However, these forms are not available at the time the tax returns are filed. Consequently, the IRS is not able to use this information to identify potentially erroneous claims when tax returns are processed. As with the Form W-2, Forms 1098-T generally do not have to be filed with the IRS until the end of March each year.

Requiring third parties such as employers and educational institutions to file information returns earlier will provide the IRS with the opportunity to use the information contained on these forms to verify tax returns at the time they are processed rather than after refunds are issued. This could significantly improve the IRS's ability to prevent the issuance of billions of dollars in erroneous tax benefits, including the EITC and education credits.

However, even if the third-party information returns are received more timely, the IRS still needs certain authorities to more efficiently and effectively use these data to address taxpayer noncompliance. Generally, the IRS must audit any tax return it identifies with a questionable claim before the claim can be adjusted or denied, even if the IRS has reliable data that indicate the claim is erroneous. However, the number of tax returns the IRS can audit is limited to available resources and the need to provide a balanced enforcement program among all taxpayer segments.

The IRS does have math error authority[38] to systemically address erroneous claims that contain mathematical or clerical errors or EITC claims with an invalid qualifying child's Social Security Number. The IRS estimates that it costs $1.50 to

---

[37] TIGTA, Audit Number 201440015, *Billions of Dollars in Potentially Erroneous Education Credits Continue to be Claimed for Ineligible Students and Institutions*, report planned for March 2015.
[38] Under current law, the IRS can adjust tax returns on which the taxpayer has made a math error utilizing summary assessment procedures.

resolve an EITC claim using math error authority, compared to $278 to conduct a pre-refund audit.

However, the majority of erroneous claims that the IRS identifies do not contain the types of errors for which it has math error authority. For example, in TY 2011, the IRS identified approximately 6.6 million potentially erroneous EITC claims totaling approximately $21.6 billion that it could not address using existing math error authority. In addition, the number of potentially erroneous EITC claims that the IRS can audit is further reduced by its need to allocate its limited resources among the various areas of taxpayer noncompliance to provide a balanced tax enforcement program. As a result, billions of dollars in potentially erroneous EITC claims go unaddressed each year.

The Department of the Treasury has included a legislative proposal to obtain correctable error authority as part of the IRS's budget requests each year since FY 2013, which would permit the IRS to disallow tax benefit claims when Government data sources do not support information on the tax return, or when taxpayers have failed to include required documentation with their tax return or exceeded the lifetime limit for claiming a deduction or credit. This authority would enable the IRS to systemically deny all tax claims for which the IRS has reliable data showing the claim is erroneous. The data available for IRS use in verifying tax returns go beyond that which is provided to the IRS on information returns such as the Form W-2.

For example, the Affordable Care Act requires Health Care Exchanges to provide data to the IRS on a monthly basis for each individual enrolled in the Exchange who purchased a qualified health insurance plan, including the amount of advance Premium Tax Credits (PTC) received. The Department of Health and Human Services estimates more than six million individuals purchased insurance through an Exchange in Calendar Year 2014. The Exchange data are available at the time tax returns are processed and can be used to ensure taxpayers have purchased insurance through an Exchange as required and have properly reconciled advance PTC payments on their tax returns before refunds are paid. However, the IRS was not given the authority to use the Exchange data to systemically disallow a PTC claim for which the data show the claim is erroneous. As a result, the IRS must audit these tax returns.

The IRS has authority to use the Department of Health and Human Services National Directory of New Hires (NDNH) which contains wage information to verify EITC claims. However, the IRS does not have the authority to systemically disallow an EITC claim that is not supported by NDNH data. Therefore, the IRS must audit the EITC claims it identifies for which NDNH data indicate the income reported is potentially erroneous. TIGTA estimates the use of correctable error authority along with expanded use of the NDNH could have potentially prevented the issuance of the more than $1.7 billion in questionable EITC claims in TY 2012 for which the IRS had no Form W-2 from an employer. TIGTA forecasted that these processes could prevent the issuance of more than $8.5 billion in potentially erroneous EITC claims over the next five years.

A similar issue also exists with education credits. To qualify for an education credit, students must attend a postsecondary educational institution that is certified by the Department of Education to receive Federal student aid funding. The Department of Education Postsecondary Education Participants System (PEPS) database includes all educational institutions certified to receive Federal student aid funding. TIGTA's comparison of TY 2012 tax returns with the Department of Education PEPS database identified more than 1.6 million taxpayers who received education credits totaling approximately $2.5 billion for students who attended institutions that are not certified to receive Federal student aid funding. As with the EITC, the IRS must audit these tax returns before the erroneous claim can be denied.[39]

Despite the IRS's numerous efforts, it is unlikely that it will achieve any significant reduction in erroneous payments without more timely access to third-party information and the ability to systemically deny erroneous claims at the time a tax return is processed. Given the scope of the improper payments that the IRS reports each year, in addition to the improper payments that remain unreported, changes in existing compliance methods could have a significant financial impact by enabling the IRS to more efficiently and effectively address this problem.

TIGTA BUDGET REQUEST FOR FY 2016

As requested by the Subcommittee, I will now provide information on our budget request for FY 2016.

TIGTA's FY 2016 proposed budget requests appropriated resources of $167,275,000, an increase of 5.7 percent from the FY 2015 enacted budget. TIGTA will continue to focus on its mission of ensuring an effective and efficient tax administration. The FY 2016 budget resources include funding to support TIGTA's critical audit, investigative, and inspection and evaluation priorities, while still maintaining a culture that continually seeks to identify opportunities to achieve efficiencies and cost savings.

---

[39] TIGTA, Audit Number 201440015, *Billions of Dollars in Potentially Erroneous Education Credits Continue to be Claimed for Ineligible Students and Institutions*, report planned for March 2015.

During FY 2014, TIGTA's combined audit and investigative efforts have recovered, protected, and identified monetary benefits totaling $16.6 billion,[40] including cost savings, increased revenue, revenue protection,[41] and court-ordered settlements in criminal investigations, and have affected approximately 3.6 million taxpayer accounts. Based on TIGTA's FY 2014 budget of $156.4 million, this represents a return on investment of $106-to-$1.

TIGTA's Audit Priorities

TIGTA's audit priorities include mitigating risks associated with tax refund fraud and identity theft, monitoring the IRS's implementation of the Affordable Care Act and other tax law changes, and assessing the IRS's efforts to improve tax compliance involving foreign financial assets and offshore accounts.

Recent audit work has shown that the IRS could develop or improve processes that will increase its ability to detect and prevent the issuance of fraudulent tax refunds resulting from identity theft. In addition, TIGTA has concerns about the security of tax data provided to the Exchanges and is also concerned that the potential for refund fraud and related schemes could increase as a result of processing ACA Premium Tax Credits.

Several key ACA provisions became effective in FY 2015, and the IRS must ensure that the tax administration system is able to fully implement these provisions. Consequently, TIGTA has implemented a multi-year audit strategy to assess the IRS's implementation of the ACA. This strategy includes coordination with other agencies, including the Department of Health and Human Services Office of Inspector General. TIGTA is conducting or planning to initiate 10 ACA-related audits during FY 2015.

The tax compliance of business and individual taxpayers involved in international transactions remains a significant concern for the IRS. Complex transfer pricing issues and identifying U.S. taxpayers with hidden foreign assets and accounts continue to demand additional IRS resources. TIGTA will continue to perform audit work to assess

---

[40] This figure includes dollars potentially compromised by bribery; dollar amount of tax liability for taxpayers who threaten and/or assault IRS employees; dollar value of resources protected against malicious loss; dollar amount of embezzlement or taxpayer remittance theft; dollar value of Government property recovered; dollar value of court ordered criminal and civil penalties, fines, and restitution; and dollar value of seizures, forfeitures, and recoveries from contract fraud.

[41] Recommendations made by TIGTA to ensure the accuracy of the total tax, penalties, and interest paid to the Federal Government.

the IRS's compliance with provisions of the Foreign Account Tax Compliance Act[42] and its efforts to improve tax compliance involving foreign financial assets and offshore accounts.

TIGTA's Investigative Priorities

TIGTA's investigative priorities include investigating allegations of serious misconduct and criminal activity by IRS employees; ensuring that IRS employees are safe and IRS facilities, data and infrastructure are secure and not impeded by threats of violence; and protecting the IRS against external attempts to corrupt or otherwise interfere with tax administration.

IRS employees are entrusted with the sensitive personal and financial information of taxpayers. It is particularly troubling when IRS employees misuse their positions in furtherance of identity theft and other fraud schemes. TIGTA will continue to proactively review the activities of IRS employees who access taxpayer accounts for any indication of unauthorized accesses that may be part of a larger fraud scheme and conduct investigations into suspected wrongdoing.

For TIGTA's investigators, our experience has shown that the IRS's expanded role under the ACA may spark a new wave of animosity directed toward IRS employees that could result in threats of violence or the actual assault of IRS employees and attacks on IRS facilities. For example, TIGTA has investigated threats made by taxpayers to IRS employees as a result of the IRS offsetting their Federal tax refunds for the repayment of student loans or court-ordered child support payments. As ACA provisions start to take effect, additional resources will be dedicated to investigating related threats.

Shortly after the Supreme Court upheld the constitutionality of the ACA, the media reported that criminals impersonated a Federal agency in an attempt to fraudulently obtain personally identifiable information from unsuspecting taxpayers. Criminals could use such sensitive information to further their identity theft schemes and other crimes under the guise that the information was required for ACA compliance. Based upon our experience investigating this type of criminal activity, TIGTA anticipates a significant increase in the number of ACA-related impersonation attempts as the IRS begins its role in ACA compliance activity.

Between FYs 2011 and 2014, TIGTA processed over 10,240 threat-related

---

[42] Pub. L. No. 111-147, Subtitle A, 124 Stat 97 (2010)(codified in scattered sections of 26 U.S.C.).

complaints and conducted over 4,990 investigations of threats made against IRS employees. TIGTA will continue to aggressively investigate individuals who threaten the safety and security of the IRS and its employees.

As mentioned earlier, the TIGTA Hotline has received over 300,000 reports from taxpayers victimized by individuals impersonating IRS employees in an effort to defraud them. As of January 31, 2015, more than 3,000 victims have reported an aggregate loss in excess of $15 million dollars. TIGTA will continue to investigate these crimes against taxpayers and alert the public to this scam to ensure that innocent taxpayers are not harmed by these criminals.

We at TIGTA are committed to our mission of ensuring an effective and efficient tax administration system and preventing, detecting, and deterring waste, fraud, and abuse. As such, we plan to provide continuing audit coverage of the IRS's efforts to operate efficiently and effectively and investigate any instances of IRS employee misconduct or fraud in IRS operations.

Chairman Boozman, Ranking Member Coons, and Members of the Subcommittee, thank you for the opportunity to share my views.

J. Russell George
Treasury Inspector General for Tax Administration

Following his nomination by President George W. Bush, the United States Senate confirmed J. Russell George in November 2004, as the Treasury Inspector General for Tax Administration. Prior to assuming this role, Mr. George served as the Inspector General of the Corporation for National and Community Service, having been nominated to that position by President Bush and confirmed by the Senate in 2002.

A native of New York City, where he attended public schools, including Brooklyn Technical High School, Mr. George received his Bachelor of Arts degree from Howard University in Washington, DC, and his Doctorate of Jurisprudence from Harvard University's School of Law in Cambridge, MA. After receiving his law degree, he returned to New York and served as a prosecutor in the Queens County District Attorney's Office.

Following his work as a prosecutor, Mr. George joined the Counsel's Office in the White House Office of Management and Budget where he was Assistant General Counsel. In that capacity, he provided legal guidance on issues concerning presidential and executive branch authority. He was next invited to join the White House Staff as the Associate Director for Policy in the Office of National Service. It was there that he implemented the legislation establishing the Commission for National and Community Service, the precursor to the Corporation for National and Community Service. He then returned to New York and practiced law at Kramer, Levin, Naftalis, Nessen, Kamin & Frankel.

In 1995, Mr. George returned to Washington and joined the staff of the Committee on Government Reform and Oversight, where he served as the Staff Director and Chief Counsel of the Government Management, Information and Technology subcommittee (later renamed the Subcommittee on Government Efficiency, Financial Management and Intergovernmental Relations), chaired by Representative Stephen Horn. There he directed a staff that conducted over 200 hearings on legislative and oversight issues pertaining to Federal Government management practices, including procurement policies, the disposition of government-controlled information, the performance of chief financial officers and inspectors general, and the Government's use of technology. He continued in that position until his appointment by President Bush in 2002.

In addition to his duties as the Inspector General for Tax Administration, Mr. George serves as a member of the Recovery Accountability and Transparency Board, a non-partisan, non-political agency created by the American Recovery and Reinvestment Act of 2009 to provide unprecedented transparency and to detect and prevent fraud, waste, and mismanagement of Recovery funds. There, he serves as chairman of the Recovery.gov committee, which oversees the dissemination of accurate and timely data about Recovery funds.

Mr. George also serves as a member of the Integrity Committee of the Council of Inspectors General for Integrity and Efficiency (CIGIE). CIGIE is an independent entity within the executive branch statutorily established by the Inspector General Act, as amended, to address integrity, economy, and effectiveness issues that transcend individual Government agencies; and increase the professionalism and effectiveness of personnel by developing policies, standards, and approaches to aid in the establishment of a well-trained and highly skilled workforce in the offices of the Inspectors General. The CIGIE Integrity Committee serves as an independent review and investigative mechanism for allegations of wrongdoing brought against Inspectors General.